Cheerful Giving
&
Kingdom Living

Cheerful Giving
&
Kingdom Living

Devotional essays reflecting
the sacredness of stewardship
with a monthly program of Planned Giving

CAROL W. BEALS

TRIANGLE BOOKS
FUQUAY-VARINA, NORTH CAROLINA

Triangle Books are published by
Research Triangle Publishing, Inc.
PO Box 1130
Fuquay-Varina, NC 27526

ISBN 1-884570-86-0

Cover Design by Kathy Holbrook

Library of Congress Catalog Card Number: 98-66205

⊖ The paper used in this publication meets the minimum requirements of the
American National Standard for Information Sciences—Permanence of Paper
for Printed Library Materials, ANSI Z39,48-1984.

Printed in the United States of America
10 9 8 7 6 5 4 3 2 1

To my husband John
and daughters
Leslie, Lynn and Laura
and their families
including our grandchildren
Hallie, Madison
and Forrest

In memory of our son
Robert (1955-1991)

In gratitude to my late parents
H. Willard and Florence Walter

To Fred Wood, Jack Kirk, Stan Banker and James Newby
Editors who gave me wings

To our First Friends Prayer Group

Dear Nelda and Larry,
In remembrance of Bob,
and in thankfulness for families
and life itself!
Blessings,
Carol
December 1998

CONTENTS

ACKNOWLEDGMENTS

To my teachers and mentors at the Earlham School of Religion, Richmond, Indiana:

Tom Mullen, professor of Creative Writing and Preaching; James R. Newby, minister of Spiritual Growth, Plymouth Congregational United Church of Christ, Des Moines, Iowa, and executive director of the D. Elton Trueblood Yokefellow Institute.

To Rodger Meier, who endowed the Patrick Henry Memorial Christian Writer's Scholarship in 1988 through the D. Elton Trueblood Academy at the Earlham School of Religion. The late Patrick Henry was for forty-one years, pastor of the Northway Christian Church in Dallas.

To the Earlham School of Religion for its nurture of Christian writers, as exemplified by its Ministry of Writing emphasis in the Quaker seminary's curriculum.

To the members and attenders of First Friends Church, Richmond, who for the last six years have generously and joyfully given to missions through the monthly program of planned giving called the Kaleidoscope of Blessings.

PREFACE

Whatever gift each of you may have received,
use it in service to one another like good stewards
dispensing the grace of God in its varied forms.
1 Peter 4:10
The New English Bible, Oxford edition

Another book on stewardship? Hasn't everything already been said about the time-honored biblical call to people of faith? Hasn't stewardship become such a routine guideline for living that we think there is nothing more to consider?

Those were questions to which I might have answered "yes" until I helped plan our church's annual budget. Ten of us faithfully spent three hours creating a fair and thoughtful financial plan for the coming year. So why did I leave that meeting feeling so dejected?

The next day as I prayed for clarity, two surprising answers came. First, following the previous night's exercise in budget making, I began to see that my view of stewardship was rigid and restricted. And second, I realized that the element of joy was missing from the deliberations of our Stewardship and Finance Committee. We were so intent on the task that we neglected to draw from the wellspring of the promises of God. That unfolding discovery led to more personal prayer and study, and eventually to writing this book.

Part One takes us over familiar territory in a new way as we examine the stewardship of time, talent, earth, and treasure. A monthly program of planned giving is presented on page nineteen to help congregations rediscover the joy of giving.

Parts Two and Three explore stewardship through the bounty of our relationships and personal experiences, where there is great treasure to be mined.

The words of Herb Mather resonate with my broadened understanding of stewardship; ". . .God calls us to be good stewards of all that we are and all that we have. . .biblical stewardship has to do with how we manage *everything* in life as a trust from God. . .it is an attitude and a way of life that cares for the whole."*

Read *my* stories; then reflect on the richness of *your* stories. And let all the facets of stewardship shine anew, illuminating your spiritual journey in fresh and exciting ways!

Carol W. Beals

*Don't Shoot the Horse ('til you know how to drive the tractor), Discipleship Resources, Nashville, Tenn., pp 5,13

Cheerful Giving
&
Kingdom Living

PART ONE

STEWARDSHIP

OF

TIME, TALENT,
EARTH & TREASURE

When you are rich in Christ,
you will know what to do with your money,
your vocation, your hobby, your life.
When you hear that voice say, "beloved,"
you will experience that same voice guiding you.

Henri Nouwen

TIME, AND TIME AGAIN

For time is a gift that you give us, Lord;
but a perishable gift, a gift that does not keep.
Michael Quoist

When our four children were small, and our family sometimes expanded with foster children or foreign students, I always stayed up late. I explained to my husband John that this was my "sanity time." Though I loved most moments of our family life, it was often hectic, even stressful. With its daily challenges, work and play, lots of laughter and occasional tears, I needed solitude to maintain personal balance. I needed time for prayer, reading (once in awhile a good mystery), writing a letter or poem, a time for reflection with God as my companion. It was as restorative as a good night's sleep.

My hunger for solitude in God's presence continues to shape my schedule. I meet the demands of family, home, church, career, and health by providing intentional spiritual spaces, seeking God's guidance and listening for direction.

A time management workshop reminded me to examine my daily "to do" list with holy scrutiny. My list usually begins with *musts* (keep an appointment with the eye doctor, pick up groceries, pay the bills); then *oughts* (answer letters, buy a birthday present, take John's shoes in for repair); and then *hopes* (invite a friend to lunch, start stitching a new wall hanging, light some logs in the fireplace and relax with Rachmaninoff).

Most days are so busy I barely work through the *musts* and only a few of the *oughts*. I rarely get to the *hopes*—the most personal part of my list. The workshop leader told us always to put near the top of our list at least one *hope*—something to satisfy the soul. Otherwise we postpone indefinitely doing that which expresses our creativity or gives us joy.

Though raised with a strong work ethic, I've learned to allow myself and others to relax without feeling anxious or guilty. Time is too precious to be a tyrant. It is a gift from God to be used carefully yet generously, for time does not keep.

THE BREAD MAN

Here is bread, which strengthens man's heart,
and therefore called the staff of life.
Matthew Henry

Every March our family gathers at Starved Rock State Park in Illinois. It is halfway between our Iowa daughter and family and the rest of us in eastern Indiana. During the three-day weekend, free from household duties, we take hikes and swim, play games, talk, relax, and enjoy each other in spontaneous ways. On Saturday we celebrate four March birthdays. In 1992, my husband John was the last of the four to open his gift.

Our children good-naturedly tease him about being the "slowest unwrapper in the Midwest." We patiently waited as he carefully pulled off the ribbon, deliberately severed the sticky tape, and methodically removed the paper. He looked at the box, musing aloud whether it actually contained what it proclaimed. It did. Our gift was a bread machine to help him celebrate his sixty-fifth birthday. Occasionally he likes to putter around in the kitchen, but his expression said he doubted what he was going to do with this contemporary contraption.

Without warning, two weeks later he was in Indianapolis having open-heart surgery. The blockages were repaired and after five days he was released to go home. Early in his recuperation, his activities were severely curtailed. He began reading the bread machine instructions. Soon he was experimenting with the recipes. It took only a few minutes plus very little energy to measure the ingredients and turn out a loaf of bread, every bit as delicious as it smelled.

As John became stronger, he kept on baking bread, giving loaves as thank-you gifts to those who had prayed for and encouraged him. He asked me to design a computer label so that each loaf would show the name of the recipient.

Six years later "John's Bread Machine Ministry" continues as he shares delicious loaves with his cardiac rehabilitation group, friends and neighbors, church members and visitors—anyone who needs to feel cared for and special.

At our church's annual bazaar, the dozen or more loaves that John bakes are sold out as soon as the doors open. Creativity and ministry are where you find them—and John's bread is especially delicious because it is made with carefully chosen natural ingredients—including love and joy.

WE HAVE ALL WE NEED

And God is able to provide you with every blessing in
abundance, so that by always having enough of everything,
you may share abundantly in every good work.
2 Corinthians 9:8 NRSV

One afternoon I was listening to the artistry of my favorite
jazz musician, pianist Marian McPartland. I felt a deep sense of
gratitude wash over me for the beauty and the beat of her music.

When music was created, had God asked us how many notes
we thought we needed, we probably would have asked for a
hundred notes, or a thousand notes, or a hundred thousand
notes, just to be on the safe side.

Instead we were given an octave, along with a few flats and
sharps, from which emerged all kinds of wonderful sacred, classical, and popular sounds and rhythms, limited only by the
skill and imagination of composers and musicians. With all its
cultural diversity, the octave continues to be enough.

My parents were top-notch musicians. Their mutual interest in music first attracted them to each other. Dad took trum-
pet lessons in school, then became a bugler in the first world
war. He continued playing for church and in dance bands. In
his forties, he took lessons, practiced faithfully, and held first
chair in three community bands. He loved to play and worked
hard to achieve a high level of proficiency.

My grandfather gave my mother a piano for her ninth birthday and hoped the music teacher next door would help her learn to play. The lessons lasted about six months when the teacher felt Mother could best progress on her own. The reason? Mother had an unerring sense of harmony flowing from her fingertips. She played classical or sacred or popular music, either sight-reading or hearing it once. The teacher encouraged Mother to practice and perfect her gifts at her own speed. As a result of this advice she became an accomplished musician. One of my fondest childhood memories is of lying in bed, hearing Mother softly playing the piano in the dark when she couldn't sleep, easily drifting from Chopin to "Deep Purple" to "Tiger Rag."

Though I took piano lessons, I had neither Mother's natural talent nor Dad's determination. Those were their particular gifts. My gift is the pleasure of listening to music, which touches me in deep places.

When I wish that I had more gifts or different gifts, then I remember the octave. God's intentions are present for each of us and the gifts we have are sufficient. Some gifts I've discovered and used well; I suspect a few are still waiting to be opened, perhaps because they are not yet needed.

In God's infinite wisdom, superb stewardship, and eternal view, each of us already has all the notes we need to create our particular music. God encourages us to keep looking for all the facets of our particular gift mix, trying new combinations, and stretching the limits of what is now understood. In fellowship, we help one another recognize each other's gifts.

As I travel along my spiritual journey, I thank God for the fullness of my octave and my particular notes—instead of asking for more.

ROUND AND ROUND WE GO

Thank you, God, for making planet earth
A home for us and ages yet unborn.
Help us to share, consider, save and store,
Come and renew the face of the earth.
Brian Wren

Earth Day twenty-five brought good news and bad news. The good news included significantly improved water and air quality in the United States. In the last six years, the national recycling rate has risen from three percent to twenty-two percent. Programs of the last twenty-five years show that we live in a time of probable natural recovery—if we are vigilant. The bad news is that emissions from greenhouse gases (mainly fossil-fuel combustion) continue to warm the planet, which may eventually disrupt agriculture. Third World countries still cannot afford to address their environmental problems. Ecological gains in the U.S. hang in the balance as both houses of Congress try to downsize government and reduce the federal deficit. This will likely result in a slippage of environmental standards. It will be more important than ever for local governments and citizens to become involved.

The testimony of simplicity was one of the reasons I was attracted to Quakerism. "Simplicity does not mean that all conform to uniform standards. Each must determine in the light that is given. . .What promotes and what hinders [the] compelling search for the Kingdom. The call to each is to abandon those things that clutter. . .life and to press toward the goal unhampered. This is true simplicity." *(Faith and Practice,* Philadelphia Yearly Meeting, 1955)

If we view the problems of our planet through the lenses of simplicity, we are shown a way to make intelligent choices. Can we do without? Can we reuse? Can we recycle? One of the best ways to thank God for the beauty and intricacy of creation is for us to take personal responsibility for amending our lifestyle.

Many of us already have developed individual habits of environmental responsibility. My early efforts were meager and haphazard, though I did turn off unused lights or running water—mostly to save money. Good idea but shortsighted motive. When ecological concerns became a matter of prayer, my turning off lights or faucets took on a new dynamic of conserving resources for someone else's future needs.

What can one individual or one family or one congregation do?

Keep an eye on local, state, national, and international pending ecological legislation, and voice your opinion by letter, telephone, or fax. I recall with gratitude the far-reaching concern and persistence of the late Sam and Miriam Levering, Quakers who initiated and influenced the Law of the Seas legislation which now protects our oceans.

Because of the environmental curriculum taught in our schools, I hope the lessons learned by today's children will carry over into adulthood.

Members of our family began recycling because of our late son Bob's example. As soon as he graduated from Earlham College in 1977 and established his own home, he became active in the Sierra Club and began to recycle on a regular basis.

In 1987 when the California State Legislature enacted a law offering refunds on aluminum cans, Bob spent several months in Huntington Beach setting up recycling centers. He viewed our planet as a trust from God—in that context, recycling became a discipline of the spirit. Out of his own faithfulness, Bob became a role model for his family and friends.

Conservation and recycling take planning, discipline, and space, and create their own kind of clutter. But each time we recycle or conserve—*planet earth breathes a sigh of relief!*

FOOD FOR THOUGHT

Is there any among you who, if your child asks for bread, will give a stone?
Matthew 7:9 NRSV

Jamie slammed the car door and dashed into the house. "Mom, we're all waiting in the car to go to church. Are you coming?"

"I'll be out in a minute," his mother called from the kitchen. "It's collection day for the food pantry and I forgot to get things together last night." *Let's see—I'll grab a couple of cans that I don't really need this week; here's one that's pretty old, might as well get rid of that; here's one with a dent—there, I guess that's enough.* "I'm coming."

"Grandma, is there anything else to eat for supper besides canned beets and bread? *Yuk!*"

"Well, Annie, that's about all we have left this week. Maybe next time the food pantry will have some more tuna or peanut butter or even canned lunchmeat. And when your Mom is well enough to go back to work, we'll celebrate by having your favorite," she smiled. "Pizza with pepperoni."

"Dad, why are you putting two of everything in the grocery cart?"

"Look, Tommy, at the top of our list, your mother wrote a reminder that this is the week we donate items to the church food pantry. I figure the families who get this food will enjoy eating the same things we do. How about handing me a couple of boxes of your favorite cereal?"

Jesus said, "Bring me the loaves and fishes, and I will bless them."

Everyone ate the same thing.

Everyone had enough.

And it was very good!

A Promise Is a Promise

Let us hold fast to the confession of our hope
without wavering,
for he who has promised is faithful.
Hebrews 10:23 NRSV

Have you read our latest church newsletter, Max?"

"I looked over it at noon, Jenny. What do you think of the faith-promise idea the church is promoting this month?"

"I guess we could try, Max. We need to decide what percent to give if we do receive any unexpected or unusual income this month. And if nothing extra comes in, I guess it means not making a contribution at all."

"I've never made a faith promise before. . .let's sleep on it, Jenny. Tomorrow we can make up our minds."

"Until yesterday I'd never heard of a faith promise, but I think I'd like to make a commitment all the same," Jenny said as she poured their breakfast coffee. "What do you think?"

"I'm willing to give it a try. . . what about ten percent?" asked Max.

"That sounds good to me," responded Jenny, "though I don't suppose anything will come of it."

❀ ❀ ❀

"Max, look what came in the mail today. It's a letter from some attorneys I've never heard of—somewhere in Toronto."

Handing him the letter, she asked, "What do you suppose it means?"

"Jenny," said Max, pausing in astonishment, "this letter says that Aunt Emma left me a bequest. Remember we got news of her death several months ago. Wow! This letter says to expect $80,000 as soon as I fill in these forms!"

"What a surprise! How generous of her! I'm glad we spent time with her last year, Max. She looked so frail, I thought that might be our last visit."

"I'm still in shock, Jenny. Maybe now we can pay off our mortgage," Max mused, "take the trip to Hawaii we've been talking about, put something in the bank to help with our grandchildren's education and. . . ."

"Before you spend it all, Max, there's something else. This is the month we agreed to faith-promise giving. That means that the first $8,000 off the top goes to our church. Of course, if the check doesn't arrive until next month maybe it wouldn't count," said Jenny, thinking aloud. "No. . .no—we promised and this is *definitely* a very unexpected source of income."

"On reflection, Jenny, I'm kind of glad this came when it did. Confined to her wheelchair the last four years, Aunt Emma could never worship in her church because of the steps. She was so pleased to see us last summer and now she has given us a special blessing. You know what? Let's designate our faith-promise gift toward our new church elevator. Out of the blue we've been given the means to help make our church accessible. And instead of adding our names to the church elevator plaque, we'll put Aunt Emma's!"

"I think I'm finally beginning to understand St. Augustine's words on the bulletin last week, Max. Do you remember? 'One loving spirit sets another on fire.' I feel Aunt Emma's loving gift igniting a new spirit of generosity in us that we can pass on to others."

Giving Until It Feels Great!

According to the Christian faith,
the deepest truth about human beings is that they are
created in the image of a generous God.
Herb Mather

Years ago, after giving our elementary school-age twin daughters their allowance of one dollar each, I offhandedly suggested that they might like to put fifty cents in the collection plate on Sundays. One of them immediately challenged my idea by asking, "Mom, do you and Dad give the church half of your money?" That probing question stayed with me as we discussed giving with our daughters, Lynn and Leslie. After our talk, both of them made a decision about how much to give to the church, each choosing a different amount.

As a result, John and I spent some time discussing our individual views of money. We talked about the wisdom we learned from our parents that we wished to continue; the blending of our differing responses to saving and spending; and lifting our resources into the Light of Christ so that both spending and saving became spiritual matters. We often included our children in these talks and were grateful to see their thoughtfulness and generosity grow as they became adults.

Many of us practice interwoven habits of stewardship—small or large economies with efficient ways of using our resources tempered by emotional and inherited views of money. John and I continued to make our finances a matter of prayer. During our early married life, and again with children in college, money was sometimes tight. It took years and a lot of prayer for us to decide to tithe. We were amazed to find that when we gave the first ten percent off the top, the remaining ninety percent was sufficient. When we answered God's call to manage both portions faithfully, there was always enough. We were on our way to a life-long growth adventure. Giving was finally beginning to feel great!

WHERE ARE ALL THE CHEERFUL GIVERS?

If you believe in something, you support it. If you support it the time comes when good wishes and cordial words are not enough and your hand reaches for your pocketbook. Then the fun begins. For giving is fun. . .If you refuse to give, your support is wavering, and if your support wavers, it can't be that you believe in something in any strong way. Maybe our account books, after all, offer the honest list of those things in which we really believe.

Kenneth Irving Brown

In the immortal words of Snoopy, "It was a dark and stormy night" in October 1991. My mood matched the weather as I drove home after our long Stewardship and Finance Committee meeting at First Friends Church. I had met with nine committed Christians whom I call my friends. We prayed for guidance, labored on next year's budget, and finally agreed on the figures. Why was I feeling so dejected? I soon retired, falling asleep counting dollar signs leaping over a pulpit.

As soon as I opened my eyes next morning, I said, "That's it!"

"What's it?" asked my husband John, in surprise.

"Now I know what was getting me down last night," I replied. "Our committee prayed and worked and completed our task, but there was no enthusiasm, no energy, no joy!"

The words "What about joy?" became a litany in my thoughts as I went about my work.

Two days later I awoke with an idea that seemed like an answer to prayer. I envisioned a way to give out of a wellspring of joy and thankfulness. I tested the idea with John, and with his encouragement talked to our pastor and the heads of committees at our church. Those contacted responded favorably. We arranged to meet in our home the next week.

When gathered, I began by sharing my concern for our church's lackluster response to giving, recalling the familiar passage, "The Lord loves a cheerful giver." Because of the diversity of the plan, I called it the Kaleidoscope of Blessings. We handed out a rough format for the program to begin in the new year. It took less than two hours to refine the original concept.

The Kaleidoscope was designed for everyone—members and attenders, all ages including young children, the homebound, nonresidents and snow birds, those with small, large or in-between income By having a different emphasis each month along with a strong motivation for generosity, we hoped our congregation could rediscover the joy of giving. Putting this plan into action was simple. We wrote brief articles for our bulletins and newsletters. Volunteers were found to give a short message during worship each month. Hundreds of return envelopes were mailed out with our newsletter and placed in the hymnals as well. By 1992 the Kaleidoscope of Blessings was ready for a trial run. Our outline for the year looked like this:

❈ JANUARY: In thankfulness to God for the gift of life as I enter a new year, I will give a matching sum for each year of my age (in any amount from one cent to ten cents to one dollar or more).

January's contributions will be given to the First Friends Food Pantry to help feed the hungry in Richmond and Wayne County, Indiana.

❀ FEBRUARY: In February, I will give a gift in honor of someone I love. If I like, I can put the initials or the name of the person(s) being honored on the Kaleidoscope envelope. These names will be put on individual paper hearts and hung on the valentine tree in the library.

February's gifts will support the Good Samaritan fund, which helps those with emergency needs.

❀ MARCH: This month, let's "fast" from buying something we think we need; instead we will give the amount of money we might have spent, but didn't.

Money collected will be used to purchase toiletries, games, and toys for an orphanage in El Salvador. Our pastor will deliver them in a few weeks when he attends a peace education seminar in Latin America.

❀ APRIL: In the spirit of Lent, during April, we are asked to sacrifice something of value, giving an equal amount to Kaleidoscope. What kind of sacrifice? We might form a car pool or walk. We might go without something we would normally buy at the grocery or drug store. We might give up a week's worth of coffee or colas. A poster is in the library for us to share our sacrifices anonymously, thus showing the creative choices of our congregation.

This month's contribution will support Christian education scholarships for our youth, enabling them to go to a United Nations seminar, a work camp with Native Americans in Alabama, or church camp.

(For the next three months we are asked to collect our loose change to be counted in July)

❀ MAY: This is an opportunity for us to give a monetary gift in memory of someone special, someone who will always have a home in our heart, If we wish, we can write the name on a leaf cutout to hang on the memory tree in the library.

May's gift will help finance the Habitat for Humanity Quaker house, being built by the three Friends churches in Richmond. Gifts of labor or lemonade and cookies for the workers are welcome, too.

(Remember to collect loose change for the next two months to be counted in July)

❀ JUNE: Scriptural examples encourage us to tithe, so this month let's see how it feels to share ten percent or more of a week's or month's income. A child with an allowance of two dollars is encouraged to give twenty cents. Adults can choose to share ten percent of either gross or net income. The gift may be made anonymously by cash or by check if credit on your financial statement is desired. For someone already tithing, an additional amount is welcome. What a gracious loving God, suggesting ten percent for Kingdom work and leaving ninety percent for us!

June's recipient is our mission hospital in Lugulu, East Africa, a ministry of Friends United Meeting. (FUM is an international body of members of the Religious Society of Friends, with headquarters in Richmond, Indiana) These funds will help pay for the installation of a pump to carry water to the operating room and hospital wards.

(Continue collecting loose change for the next month to be counted in July)

❀ JULY: This is the time to continue saving our loose change until the last Sunday in July. Then bring coins (or an equivalent check if coins are too heavy) on the last Sunday. A wheelbarrow provided by Barker's Fireplace Shop will be located in the church library for the collection of coins. After worship, the loose change will be gathered, blessed, and the children will sort the coins. Our treasurer will take them to the bank on Monday to be counted and wrapped.

July's contribution will be given to the local Home for the Battered, where several of our members volunteer. Let our loose change represent a measure of peace standing up to violence in our community.

❁ AUGUST: We are invited to give a matching sum equal to the cost of one or two summer recreational activities. Send in a sum equal to the cost of dining out, an overnight in a motel, the price of a video, movie, or golf game. Let's have fun and remember Kaleidoscope.

Think of how hot it is in the Cabrini-Green inner city apartments in Chicago in the summer. Our money will help the Chicago Fellowship of Friends, a ministry of Friends United Meeting, raise funds for its scholarship ministry project. This enables young people to spend two weeks on a farm for a welcome change of pace.

❁ SEPTEMBER: We are asked to make a Faith Promise this month. A Faith Promise is a covenant between God and us to tithe a portion of any unexpected income that comcs our way. A refund, an inheritance, a dividend, or a monetary gift might be this type of income.

September's contributions will help pay for our recently installed elevator. Memorial gifts are flowing in, but more are needed. Let's make the elevator debt go down, while our members ride up—to our worship room and fellowship hall.

❁ OCTOBER: Here's a chance for us to spend a month creating and collecting items for sale at our craft fair to be held the first Saturday in November. Food, needlework, wood, metal and fabric crafts—if you make them we'll sell them.

Proceeds will pay for books and materials for our Christian education classes. The money also will pay babysitters for the nursery, so our members can attend worship or sing in the choir.

❁ NOVEMBER: We are asked to give a gift in gratitude for someone or something. A Thanksgiving poster is hung in the library to write names or events which we honor.

The money will purchase craft supplies and games for an orphanage in Richmond's Sister City in Serpukhov, Russia. Our pastoral administrative assistant is traveling there next month and will personally deliver our gifts and greetings.

❁ DECEMBER: This month, let's honor the birth of the Christ child. Imagine following the star and laying a gift at the foot of the manger.

Our contributions will help rebuild the Ramallah Play Center in the West Bank in the Middle East following last month's bombing. When Christ walked this land, he said, "Let the children come unto me." Our gift offers the refugee children a respite in their war-weary country.

The prayerful and generous response to the Kaleidoscope of Blessings was whole-hearted. A young teacher said that she felt a sense of anticipation as each month's cause was announced. A businessman told our pastor that the Kaleidoscope made him open his heart as well as his checkbook. A nonresident member living in Arizona sent a modest dividend check quarterly, writing that she finally felt connected to her home church in Indiana.

The Kaleidoscope of Blessings continues to be renewed each year. The giving has increased, with more than $12,000 collected outside the budget. Each year we add new recipients and new challenges. Recent religious polls show that people like to know where their money is going. Kaleidoscope's focused approach nurtures generosity.

And at last, at First Friends, we are giving with joy!

PART TWO

STEWARDSHIP
OF
RELATIONSHIPS

The thread of our life would be dark,
Heaven Knows! If it were not with
friendship and love intertwine'd.

Thomas Moore

A CHRISTMAS STOCKING

Death may end a life but does not end a relationship.
Stephen Levine

Starting with the birth of our twin daughters, hanging Christmas stockings became a family tradition. The stockings took on additional significance about twelve years ago, when our son Bob, after looking at the mountain of unopened gifts, suggested that next year all the adults exchange names. We readily agreed. It simplified shopping, was less expensive, and gave us more time to bake cookies, go caroling, and visit friends and family.

We decided to put small handmade or inexpensive gifts into the stockings of those whose names we did not draw. The pleasure of finding just the right gift became a further source of showing love for one another, and welcoming the Christ child.

Ordinarily on my birthday, December third, we brought out the crèche, put up the tree, decorated our home, and hung the stockings. But in 1991, it was hard to get into the spirit of Christmas, Our beloved son Bob, who battled leukemia for three years, had died in early April—finally peace for him; leaden hearts for us. I recalled Bob's final Christmas, after we had opened our gifts. I watched his hands, pale and translucent from chemotherapy, methodically roll up his empty stocking. I tried to hide my tears. Unless there was a miracle, he wouldn't be with us next Christmas. And the miracle for which we all prayed and longed for did not come.

Our three daughters, Leslie, Lynn, and Laura, came over to help us prepare for the holidays. I told them everything was done, except hanging the Christmas stockings. In the drawer of the antique cherry chest were nine stockings, one for each member of our enlarged family, including two little grand-daughters. I couldn't bear to take eight stockings out, leaving one alone in the drawer. "Mom," said one of our girls, "we have an idea. See what you and Dad think of it." We listened, smiled in agreement, and brought out *all* the stockings.

My husband John fastened eight hooks to the front of the mantel, and another one unobtrusively around the corner. All the stockings were hung, with Bob's at one end. Following our daughters' plan, during the month of December, we all put money into Bob's stocking. Then on Christmas Eve, his three sisters and his dad and I decided on a recipient. The first year we gave a sizable gift anonymously to a friend who was having a tough time financially. The next year we gave a gift to leukemia research. The following Christmas it was sent to Habitat for Humanity, a long-time interest of our son's. Last year we gave it to a friend from church, accompanied by a let-ter of encouragement as he made a difficult life-changing de-cision. And each succeeding year we've discovered some urgent need that can be met by the gift in Bob's stocking.

That year, as we talked about the gift, our five-year-old grand-daughter was busy coloring nearby. Later when we emptied Bob's stocking to count the money, we found a surprising "contribu-tion" that made five adults weep—a yellow piece of paper with laboriously-made capital letters that said I LOVE YOU, UNCLE BOB. HALLIE.

We once again look forward to hanging the stockings as part of our welcome to the Babe in the manger. It's also a time to thank God for the thirty-five years we shared with Bob; to re-call his capacity for enjoying each day, and to remember his interest and concern for family, friends, and students. Filling his stocking is a way for us to extend his spirit of generosity.

This new Christmas tradition moves us along our grief jour-ney yet helps us stay connected—for a loving relationship does not conclude with death.

THE WORLD AT OUR TABLE

*Friendship is the only cement that will
ever hold the world together.*
Anonymous

Some of our most memorable friendships are of short duration. I think of the college students from Japan and British Guyana who stayed with us when the dorms were closed. Or the high school student from West Germany who spent his senior year with us through the Youth for Understanding program. It was the late '60s and early '70s. We learned so much about family life, religion, education, and politics in other cultures. We learned about the personal hopes and dreams of our "sons" as they pursued education in America. In turn, they learned about life in the United States, about the daily hustle-bustle of a family of six plus one, and about our Quaker faith. It was the high point of our day as we gathered for our evening meal and held hands to say grace. Much learning took place around our table.

There was Tets—Tetsuya—a long way from Japan. There was an elegance about him, a shy sense of humor, and an eagerness to soak up the atmosphere in our home.

One Saturday, he asked John to take him to see the city's train station. John said, of course, but told Tets he might be disappointed because trains no longer stopped in Richmond and the depot was boarded up. Tets looked unconvinced so he and John made the ten-minute ride to the depot. Tets got out of the car, went over to the empty weed-ridden tracks, looked up and down, and went back to the boarded-up depot, shaking his head in wonder. The only signs of life were pigeons flying in and out of broken windows.

In disbelief, he got into the car. On the way home Tets explained to John that Tokyo was a city whose people and trains were always on the move—trains were the heartbeat and hub of his city. He couldn't understand how we got along without them. We said that autos, buses, planes, and semi-trucks had taken their place. Once in awhile, referring to the deserted depot, he said morosely, "Poor little Richmond—not a train in sight."

Tets was wonderful with our young children—playful, yet treating each one with the utmost respect. His dexterity as he performed after-dinner magic tricks was amazing. Paper flowers, fish, and birds appeared and disappeared, fluttering lightly through his fingers, mesmerizing our children and us.

After a year in the States, Tets returned to Tokyo to pursue his dream of becoming a journalist.

Alec spent two Christmases and many weekends with us. He came to Earlham College from British Guyana, hoping to become a teacher like his father. His mother was a homemaker; Alec was the second oldest of eleven children and the first to be educated in the U.S.

Liking to pad around in his stocking feet, Alec often talked to me while I was cooking. I tried to imagine his family at the dinner table—thirteen lively, intelligent people with British accents and stimulating conversation, if they were anything like Alec. He had a favorite saying, so oft repeated that it grated on my nerves—"*It's the thought that counts.*" One evening he was puzzled because I was not cooking at the usual time. I invited him to sit beside me. "Alec, you always say it's the thought that counts. Let's think about dinner!" He grinned, got the message, and even offered to help me cook.

Early in December, Alec began preparing a Christmas tape to send to his family. He wanted the six of us to introduce ourselves, and sing or say something personal so his family could get to know us.

Alec started the tape, naming his family, one by one, and then we sent our greetings, one by one. Unfortunately, each of us, except John, got the giggles when we couldn't find the starting note of our song, or couldn't remember what we were going to say. An increasingly frustrated Alec erased our part of the tape, and in a contrite manner our family would begin again. Finally, on the fourth take, we made a reasonable presentation. Alec left the room saying he wanted to listen to it in its entirety before taking it to the post office.

He returned shortly, with a long face, and asked us sweetly, with great humility, if we would try one more time. In his original family greeting he had neglected to include his nine-year-old brother Cecil in the family line-up. Midst great hilarity, with Alec joining in, we finally got it right—the fifth time round!

Alec moved to Ohio to work on his master's degree and went home to Guyana to teach English.

Thomas lived with us for a year in 1968-69, attending Richmond High School as a senior. A native of Hamburg, West Germany, Tom, a six-foot-five blond, had a keen intellect and lots of questions about his new home in Indiana. A gifted musician, it was a joy to listen to the strains of Bach and Mozart coming from his flute. He fitted easily into the lifestyle of our family of six, and his fluency in English improved daily.

Shortly before graduation, he was invited to give the Sunday morning message at our Friends church. He thanked everyone for the warmth of hospitality he had received. He added that he had been greatly influenced by living with a Quaker family and attending a Quaker church. As a result he intended to become a peace activist when he returned to West Germany. With a tremor in his voice, he leaned into the microphone and said, "I have a father in Hamburg whom I love, and a father in Richmond whom I love." Looking at John, he continued, "and I do not want to live in a world where my two fathers might someday shoot at one another!"

Returning to his homeland, Tom immediately entered college, and now is a practicing psychiatrist in Freiburg, Germany.

Tets, Alec, and Tom enriched our family, expanded our circle of love, and brought the world to our table.

Saying Goodbye. . .Slowly

*The pain we feel over losing the presence of a person
is a reminder of the value of what we've been given.*
Marti Lynn Matthews

The phone rang in the family room; my husband John answered. After a pause I heard his murmured words of consolation. He came into the kitchen saying, "That was Elaine; Jim died this evening. All of the family was with him. She'll call back when the service is arranged." Jim and Elaine—dear friends for many years over many miles. . . .

Jim grew up on an orchard in Oregon, then went away to college, still undecided as to a career. After graduation, he felt a call to the ministry. When he enrolled in a midwestern seminary, John and I became acquainted with him and Elaine, first through a prayer fellowship group. Later on our friendship deepened when the four of us went on a work camp to Jamaica to help build a parsonage in the Blue Mountains.

After seminary Jim and Elaine moved back west, where he began his pastorate near his boyhood home. We kept in touch with them and their four young daughters with occasional letters and telephone visits. With busy family schedules, our connection dwindled down to holiday notes and photos. One Christmas we learned that our friends had returned to manage the orchard following the death of Jim's dad. Several years later a note told us that the orchard had been sold, Jim had begun a new pastorate, and Elaine now worked in a bank. Their daughters had all gone off to college or careers.

Still later Elaine began to write of Jim's intermittent memory losses, with the subsequent diagnosis of Alzheimer's. He could no longer serve as pastor or hold any other kind of a job. For a while he stayed alone at home while Elaine was at work, but at year's end another Christmas message shared the news that Jim now required day care for his protection and Elaine's peace of mind.

Everyone in the day care facility loved Jim—in his lucid moments he ministered professionally and tenderly to both patients and staff. Ten months later round-the-clock nursing care became a necessity. . . .

In 1994, John and I decided to take a long-dreamed-of vacation to the Northwest. We called a delighted Elaine to plan time together.

The first two days passed quickly as we did lots of catching up. Our last day together Elaine asked if we would like to come with her to visit Jim at the care facility where he had spent the last nine years. I said yes, though I wasn't sure what to expect. John hesitated, frankly saying he didn't know if he could bear to see his old friend in this setting.

After a half-hour drive, we came to a neatly landscaped brick building. John paused for a moment of decision and then followed Elaine and me through double doors and a maze of hallways. We entered a cheerfully painted room with twenty or so patients in hospital lounge chairs. I immediately saw Jim—that same handsome Jim, now with graying hair—but no expression in his eyes. Elaine took his hand, telling him that he had some visitors from Indiana. He did not respond. I stroked his arm and said, "Jim, there are lots of people back in Indiana who remember you and send their love." Again, no response. Then John moved nearer to Jim and taking his hand began to speak. Suddenly Jim gripped John's wrist, holding it so tight that it was painful, and Jim's eyes bored into John's (as John said later, "into my very soul"). And for the first time Jim uttered a brief unintelligible message. Was it an uncanny reflex or momentary unlocked fragment of memory?

Six weeks later Jim died.

Whenever we relive that intense encounter, as we often do, we count it a gift from God—God's benediction on friendship!

CHOICES OF THE HEART

What is a friend? A single soul dwelling in two bodies.
Aristotle

Except for my husband, my relatives are inherited. I love all of them and like most of them. However, friends are different—either we choose them or they choose us. How long we stay in relationship depends upon our nurture or neglect. Miles don't matter as long as souls connect.

Usually we are attracted to someone because we have similar interests or experiences. We remain friends because there is a personal connection or something we admire. I really admire persistence, which is often in short supply for me. Let me tell you about my friend D'Ann from New Jersey.

We were sophomores at Earlham College living in the same dorm and we were good buddies. One Thursday evening she dropped by my room around 8 p.m. I was already in my pajamas.

"Carol, I'm on my way to the Commons (our campus meeting place) and I'd like you to go with me."

"Oh, D'Ann, I'm ready for bed and I've got to read forty more pages before my 8 a.m. class tomorrow," I said, holding up the *Streams of Civilization* textbook that was making me drowsy. "I'll go with you this weekend, if you like, but not tonight," I said firmly. "Why don't you ask Barb?"

"She just shampooed her hair and it's not dry yet," replied D'Ann.

"How about Corky?" I asked.

"She has a date."

Before I could suggest someone else, D'Ann said, "Mabel's at play rehearsal, Maggie's practicing the piano, and June is having a late dinner with her parents."

"Why tonight?" I asked, growing weary of the debate.

"I met a terrific guy in band this afternoon. His name is Paul and he plays the clarinet. He and a friend are going to be in the Commons tonight and he hopes I'll come, too. But I don't want to go alone."

"Well, ask Bev or Amy or Connie. I'll bet one of them would go with you. Good luck," I smiled, trying to renew interest in my assignment.

Ten minutes later D'Ann returned, standing in my doorway dejectedly. "Bev's in bed with a cold, and the other two are out. Please, Carol. Please, please, please," she wheedled.

"All right, all right," I said distractedly. "Give me a few minutes to get dressed. But I'm only going to stay for an hour—no longer!"

We took the shortcut down the fire escape and crossed over to the Commons. Lights were bright, the jukebox was playing but on a weeknight the place was nearly empty. Four students were playing ping-pong, and two young men were sitting in a booth. One was blond and the other brunette. "Which one is Paul?" I whispered. "The blond," she whispered back. "Who is the other one?" "I don't know his name, but he plays cornet in the band."

The two men, both well over six feet, stood up as we neared the booth. We sat down and introductions were made—D'Ann, Carol, Paul, and John. We chatted for awhile. Then John, probably with instructions from Paul, asked me if I would like to play ping-pong. I agreed. We signed out paddles and balls, and played three competitive games, fairly evenly matched. We returned to the booth.

Looking meaningfully at D'Ann, I said, "I've really got to get back to the dorm now to study." Silence. John and I stood there, getting dark looks from D'Ann and Paul.

"I'll walk you back to the dorm, Carol, if you like," John offered.

"I'll take D'Ann back to the dorm later," said Paul. Smiles from D'Ann and Paul.

John and I left the Commons, chatting on the brief walk to Earlham Hall. He was a day student who worked a forty-hour-a-week job to pay his tuition. Tonight was his first visit to the Commons. I told him I was from Indianapolis, thought I'd like to become a journalist, and that I worked part-time in the library to help with expenses. We said goodnight on the dorm steps. He went home to study for a Spanish vocabulary test and I went upstairs to tackle *Streams of Civilization* once again.

That was the night I met the man who has been my husband for forty-eight years. D'Ann and Paul, on the other hand, had one date, and decided they had nothing in common but the clarinet.

D'Ann, still my friend today, has many wonderful qualities. But the one I admire the most is persistence!

One of my dearest friends was once my editor and my supervisor. Twenty-eight years ago I was interviewed for part-time work with *Quaker Life* magazine. Fred was the editor and I was hired to be his assistant. We worked well together, enjoying the stimulation and challenge of co-creating a monthly religious journal for Friends United Meeting. We laughed about the mistakes found while proofreading *before* the magazine went to the printer, and commiserated over tardy writers who failed to meet their deadlines. This congenial working relationship lasted for eight years until his retirement. By then Fred, his wife Betty, and John and I were good friends. We attended the same Friends church and often socialized together.

Betty began to experience heart problems about the same time that our son Bob was diagnosed with leukemia. Three years later, near the end of March, Betty died, just a few weeks after our last visit with her. Word came to us while we were in Cincinnati at the bedside of our son, who died the first of April. Though unable to attend Betty's memorial service, we sent Fred word of our abiding love and sympathy for his loss.

Four days later, at our son's memorial service, Fred spoke movingly about his remembrance of Bob. One breaking heart comforting another!

Some friends leave us too soon, but a relationship does not end with death. My college roommate Barbara died six years ago of lymphoma. We were good friends for forty-seven years, though she lived in Vermont and I in Indiana. She was married to Howard, and we were honor attendants for each other's weddings. They had five children and we had four. We kept in touch through visits, phone calls, letters, and photos.

Neither of us had a sister, so during our college years Barb and I filled that role for one another. She had a perceptive mind, a charitable heart, and a wry philosophy of life. I would have gladly exchanged metabolisms with her—I was always dieting unsuccessfully; she had the appetite of a stevedore and remained slender all her life. Though our personalities differed, we were often on the same spiritual wavelength. Both active in campus Christian fellowship groups, we shared deep feelings about our personal spiritual journeys. Her faith, both apparent and transparent, illuminated the faith journey of others on campus.

A few weeks before her death, we spoke on the phone. Her last words were, "Please pray for me." And I did. I prayed that she would be comforted and cuddled in God's loving arms and given peace. And she was.

The depth of her faith is a beacon to me still!

As for the rest of my friends, I hope some day to write your stories. . . .

When I think of you as I often do, I recall Robert Southey's words: *No distance of place or lapse of time can lessen the friendship of those who are thoroughly persuaded of each other's worth.*

The Brady Bunch

If we loved one generation of children, all of the world's problems would disappear because a loved person doesn't hurt self or neighbor.
Bernie Siegel

Once a year my friend Karen and I drive 200 miles from each of our homes to spend a long weekend together, relaxing from the pressures of our careers—she, a clinical social worker, and I, an editor for a religious magazine. We stay at a state park and enjoy unhurried time together. We hugged each other in anticipation. We settled into adjoining rooms, and met on the balcony to sip cups of tea. It was a mid-September afternoon, filled with summer's warmth. Breaking the silence, I voiced a thought that had niggled at me while I was driving.

"Every time I feel stressed out at work, I think of you, Karen, especially now that you spend all your time counseling families involved in abuse. Faith plays a big part in both our lives and professions, but with counseling sessions, court appearances, and daily contact with victims of abuse, how do you keep hope alive?"

Thoughtfully Karen responded. "Most days are difficult. We live in a pleasant small town with educational, cultural, and civic opportunities, lively congregations, able leaders, and many

decent people. However in my work, I see the underside of
the rock. Sometimes I get discouraged with an overworked
and indifferent legal system. I feel anger at the nonstop violence one person inflicts on another, especially on children.
But whenever it all seems hopeless I remember the BRADY
bunch."

Puzzled, I asked, "Isn't that the name of an old TV show
with six kids? I remember hearing it while our four children
watched. I was usually preparing dinner and wishing I had a
live-in housekeeper named Alice too! But what does that have
to do with hope?"

Karen smiled at my quizzical expression. "For more than
four years I counseled five children whose family also included
a mother and assorted fathers. As I jotted down the children's
names, I noticed that their initials—Brad, Robbie, Angela,
Derek, and Yvonne—spelled BRADY. From then on I could
never shake the connection.

"The mother was a stony-faced woman, undoubtedly the vic-
tim of abuse herself. The children, each fathered by a different man, ranged in age from nine to three. The mother's
current companion, related to none of the children, was an
abuser who defied authorities and refused counseling. The
children, when not in school, sat transfixed with the TV as
babysitter, while their mother 'entertained.'

"Brad was the protector who carried enormous responsibili-
ties on his nine-year-old shoulders. As eldest and strongest,
he suffered mostly verbal abuse. In one of his sessions, Brad
shared a recurring dream. 'I have a pet dog, big and shaggy,
named Wolf. Whenever Mom or her friend starts in on one of
us, all I have to do is yell "Wolf." The dog attacks the grownups
and makes them stop doing whatever they're doing. But,' he
added, 'Wolf's always friendly to us kids.'

"Robbie showed signs of autism. He hummed as he moved
his body back and forth. He took no interest in his surround-

ings, except when he thought no one was looking. Then his eyes darted around taking in everything, quickly going blank when he was noticed. In time counseling revealed that he was imitating an autistic child he saw in a special ed. class at his school. He figured out that if he acted weird, his mom and her friends might leave him alone.

"Angela, at six, was world weary. Molested with her mother's consent most of her life, she had no conscience. Her eyes looked dead. She cared for no one. If she didn't feel, she didn't hurt.

"Derek at four was both shy and sickly. His frequent attacks of asthma frightened him. When he needed attention, his mother was nowhere to be found. Usually Brad gave him his medicine. His illness set him apart from the others. Abuse always triggered his asthma.

"Yvonne, nearly three, hardly spoke. The message in her eyes said it all. She cringed when spoken to and trusted no one—her mother, her siblings, or strangers like me who tried to help."

"But Karen, I don't see any rainbows here," I responded.

"It all started when neighbors reported the neglect and abuse of these children to the Welfare Department. I was assigned to the case and counseling began. I accompanied these damaged children to court for custodial hearings. After months of working through red tape, the parental rights of the mother were terminated and the children were placed with five foster families."

"Did things improve?" I asked.

"Not really. At this time in their lives, they trusted no one. They missed one another and they even missed the familiar chaos of their former home. Once in awhile Angela would ask if they would see their mom again, dreading the answer. Their progress at school and day care improved slightly, but none were at ease in their foster homes.

"I still don't see real signs of hope here, Karen," I persisted.

"As I counseled the children for several years, they gradually began to open up. The older ones missed the younger children, for they rarely saw one another. They were fairly stable at school and Derek's asthma was under control, but none felt at home with foster family life.

"One day Derek's foster parents, Dave and Esther, called for an appointment. I had never met them. I wondered if they had found Derek's asthma too much to cope with and wanted him to leave. They came into my office, a middle-aged couple who lived on a farm, and told me what they had in mind. Parents of six grown children, they had been foster parents to dozens of youngsters in the last fifteen years. With an empty nest, except for Derek, they wanted to become foster parents to Derek's siblings as well! I was amazed and grateful for their generous offer and the thought of those five children, longing to be together.

"After some sessions with Dave and Esther and the children, the placement was approved. The early months were stressful as the children became reacquainted, and tested the limits of new home and school environments. Counseling continued. The children seemed more settled, but not yet trusting.

"A year and a half later, Dave and Esther requested another appointment with me. What's up now, I thought, just when we seemed to be making some gains! I greeted them wondering what they had to say.

"Esther spoke first. 'These last two years have been difficult. Each of the children continues to react to their unsavory beginnings in different ways. Their trust level is low. They wake each day surprised at still being in our home. Even though they are in a safe place, memories of violence and abuse still color their thoughts.'

"Dave spoke up with a smile. 'At the same time, I think we're making real progress. I think there is cause for optimism. So we are wondering,' looking first at his wife and then at me, 'if we could begin adoption proceedings for all five.'

'Our children are all on their own now,' said Esther. 'We have lots of room for these children. Every once in awhile we see a flicker of hope. We have prayed about this and think that the only way for them to learn to trust and to love is for them to be together permanently.'

"I was awed by their generosity and understanding. After lots of paper work, interviews, and home visits, adoption proceedings moved forward," Karen related. "The children were at first suspicious, then unbelieving and finally surprised to be wanted. Their reactions emerged at different rates. As the counseling sessions became less frequent, the children became more willing to talk.

"Brad no longer seemed like a little old man—finally someone else was taking care of his brothers and sisters—and him. He no longer needed a dream pet, for the family dog, Rusty, became his special pal. He looked forward to doing after-school chores with his new dad.

"Robbie, insisting on the new name of 'Rob' for himself, gradually gave up his weird behavior, no longer wanting to be ignored. He proved to be a slow but receptive student, willing to do his homework and help around the farm.

"I sometimes wonder if Angela's feeling of self-hate will ever go away. Less withdrawn, she works hard to make passing grades. At home it's as if old memories make it hard for her to relate to her siblings. Once in awhile she giggles like the little girl she never was. She complains about chores, but likes to bake cookies.

"Derek, his asthma now under control, no longer relies on his illness to escape abuse. In first grade he has two new friends. He enjoys feeding the chickens and singing in Sunday school.

"Yvonne, too young to understand the violent outbursts in her former life, recoiled from any touch in the early days with her new family. Gradually as her mother helped her put on her shoes and socks, she began to relax and accept an occasional hug. Now in kindergarten, she works hard to deal with a learning disability. She eagerly runs from the school bus to show Esther her papers. After a snack, she helps set the table—carefully counting out sets of seven for the evening meal. She finally believes she's in a safe place."

"Wow, that's quite a story! Do you still keep in touch?"

"Counseling continued for another year with fewer appointments," Karen continued. "The children flourished at different rates, slowly learning to trust two adults who are kind but firm in their expectations.

"Each spring I receive a note from Esther. The family experiences the usual ups and downs associated with child-rearing Overall life is pretty good on the farm."

We finished our tea and watched the sun shimmering on golden leaves.

Karen continued. "Especially at Easter I think about the BRADY bunch—of the death of a destructive lifestyle and the resurrection within a new family. The memory of God's grace is with me as I go about my work and pray for my clients. That is my source for hope. When things are rough, I remember the BRADY bunch. It keeps me going!"

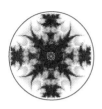

PART THREE

STEWARDSHIP
OF
EXPERIENCES

Everything that happens to you is your
teacher. The secret is to learn to sit at the feet
of your own life and be taught by it.
Everything that happens is either a blessing
which is also a lesson, or a lesson
which is also a blessing.

Polly Berrien Berends

CIGARETTES ON THE ALTAR

*For we do not have a high priest who is unable to
sympathize with our weaknesses, but have one who in
every respect has been tested as we are, yet without sin.*
Hebrews 4:15 NRSV

Gathered on Sunday morning, we were settling expectantly
into the familiar rhythm of worship. Though torrents of rain
poured outdoors, the sanctuary was filled with a kind of inner
radiance as we sang "Morning Has Broken." A chapter from
Matthew was read and a brief prayer was given. The children's
message was shared with eleven wiggly yet attentive little ones.
Next, familiar strains of Bach came from the organ to usher in
the offertory. Our pastor's message deepened the sense of
God's presence among us. Then we paused for silent meditation and reflection.

A young man in jeans, plaid shirt, and sandals quietly pad-
ded down the aisle—many of us recognized him as a resident
from a nearby group home. Several months ago when three
group home residents began to worship with us, they were a
minor distraction. But now we knew their names and were
accustomed to seeing them on Sunday mornings. However,
an interruption during worship was unusual. The young man

beckoned to our pastor Alan and whispered for a moment, and they spoke quietly for several more.

Standing beside the young man, Alan turned to the congregation. "Our friend Dennis wants us to pray with him that he can give up smoking. He wants to place this almost empty pack of cigarettes on the altar, asking God to help him break the habit."

Heads once again bowed, we prayerfully focused on Dennis' request. After a few moments, Alan spoke again: "Each one of us has something to lay on the altar to be bathed in Christ's healing light—as each one of us prays for Dennis, we pray for all."

An invisible yet tangible energy rippled through the congregation. I knew that in Heaven's view, the altar was heaped high with heartfelt prayers—and on the very top was an almost empty pack of cigarettes.

Getting It Right/The First Time

*The task Your wisdom has assigned here let me
cheerfully fulfill; in all my work Your presence first and
prove Your good and perfect will. . .and labor on at Your
command, and offer all my work to You. . . .*
Charles Wesley

The year was 1990. Reclining uneasily in the dental chair, I handed Dr. Cameron the large filling that had recently fallen out. Dismayed at its size and condition, he said, "We'll X-ray your molar, Carol, but I'm certain the rest of your tooth will have to come out. I doubt that it can be refilled."

Trying not to be anxious, I reviewed my pitiful "tooth history" while I waited. . . .

My uncle, my mother's brother, was my dentist until I married and moved away from Indianapolis. His office and waiting room were in his home. Highly respected in his profession, his patients loved him. For many years he made dentures in his own lab; his articles were published in medical journals, and he held several patents for advanced dental procedures. I loved him, too—outside of his office.

Uncle Bob enjoyed working on my dad. We always heard cordial conversation and laughter coming from the next room.

However, with his usual candor, my uncle admitted my mother and I were not his favorite patients. In the vernacular of the '30s, he said we were both "panty waists." And we probably were! Mother and I undoubtedly left lasting imprints on the arms of the chair—with our pre-fear, mid-fear, and post-fear (in case he wasn't yet finished).

Twice yearly check-ups were an ordeal for us—and for him. I pretty much subscribed to my mother's philosophy about dentistry. Though a woman of common sense and uncommon faith, just before an appointment she would shake her head sadly and say, "Sometimes I think God was having an off-day when teeth were created."

In those pre-fluoride days I had a predisposition to cavities, causing me to endure a number of drilling and filling sessions. One summer in Jamaica on a work camp, I lost a filling from a molar, chewing some tropical unknown. Living in a charming but primitive village, the horrific thought of going to a strange dentist in a strange country forced me to put up with intermittent pain until I got back to the States.

In September, I made an appointment with my uncle, who scolded me for waiting so long as he once again drilled and filled. With my mouth stretched an inch beyond its normal elasticity, the task took more than an hour. That was in 1949. . . .

Dr. Cameron returned with my X-ray and a big grin. "I have some good news. I don't know who your dentist was or how long ago this filling was put in, but the foundation below the filling was done so well, that I think I can save the tooth. You won't need an extraction after all."

By this time I was smiling, too, and thanking God that my late uncle got it right the first time—forty-one years ago!"

GETTING IT RIGHT/
THE THIRD GENERATION

Therefore whosoever heareth these sayings of mine,
and doeth them, I will liken him unto a wise man,
which built his house upon a rock. And the rain descended and
the floods came, and the winds blew, and beat upon that house
and it fell not, for it was founded upon a rock.
Matthew 7:24-25 KJV

Named for his great-uncle, our son Bob had an insatiable curiosity about anything and everything. As he grew up, he was eager to learn more and to teach others. From an early age Bob spent hours with his grandfathers—both builders—who taught him respect for tools and wood as well as basic building skills. From one grandmother he learned about birds and plants and animals. From his other grandmother he developed a love for music and harmony and the finer points of chess. With his dad he discovered the joys of camping and fishing, as well as rudiments of land surveying and auto mechanics. And from me, he found enjoyment in the gift of hospitality.

When Bob moved to Cincinnati to begin his teaching career, he purchased an old house to remodel. One hundred years ago it belonged to a prominent family. A three-story frame dwelling, it had a broad front stairway to the second floor, and a narrow rear staircase going to the third floor. By the time Bob became owner, the house had been cut up into five cramped and decrepit apartments.

He began by clearing out the third floor, living there while he "rehabbed" the first floor for his permanent home. He remodeled the third floor and then the second, turning them into attractive rentals. He added an outside stairway to meet codes and add privacy.

Highly disciplined, he studied books on building techniques, made detailed plans for each space, and followed a weekly work schedule. A dedicated elementary teacher, he always left time for relaxation, with hiking, having dinner with friends, playing the guitar, and going to jazz concerts rating high priority. Sometimes his friends and family pitched in to help him achieve the home of his dreams. He maintained high standards for renovation each step of the way, and was always willing to teach others. Although the restoration took several years, the transformation resulted in spacious rooms with their original high ceilings, polished woodwork, and elegant stained glass windows.

(While this devotional shares his usual *modus operandi,* I think of two times when miscalculations taught Bob valuable lessons. The first concerned the outdoor stairway, which he constructed on the ground. He underestimated by one person the number it would take to lift it into place. Only God's grace and a burst of extraordinary strength kept it from falling. His second lesson came when he traded in some sluggish shares of stock in an athletic company—sixteen months before Reeboks became the rage. Hanging on to those would have paid off the mortgage much sooner!)

Anyone who has embarked on remodeling knows that one of the most tedious tasks is putting up dry wall. The sheets are heavy, and the nailing, taping, "mudding" (spreading wet plaster to fill in all the nooks and crannies), and sanding seem to go on forever. Bob held to his standards here, too. When looking at his walls and ceiling, there were no "dimpled" nail holes to reproach him for a job poorly done.

Now, seven years after his death at age thirty-five from leukemia, his personal standards linger. His family and friends have all had the same experience—whatever job we tackle, we feel Bob's presence, offering encouragement and reminding us "to plan ahead, measure twice, cut once, and get it right—the first time."

His family and friends thank God for the qualities of several generations that emerged in Bob. And often I find myself praying, "Please, God, help me get it right—the first time!"

Seeking and Finding

Then when you call upon me and come and pray to me,
I will hear you. When you search for me, you will find me;
If you seek me with all your heart.
Jeremiah 29:12,13 NRSV

These words from Jeremiah offer a message of personal hope. Our lives involve not only a journey but also a search—one that leads to God and at the same time is with God.

The magnificence of the search lies in the fact that we have no visible chart mapping our lives. Rather the search is clouded in mystery—leaving us with the expectation that through prayer, worship, reading of the Scriptures and other valuable writings, meditation and personal reflection, as well as fellowship with other seekers, signposts will appear to direct our spiritual discovery.

The search is lifelong—always stimulating, often surprising. God is revealed to us in many ways and rejoices when we share our stories with one another.

The mystery of life is a gift for which I am truly thankful. If everything were spelled out ahead of time, we might hurry toward that which is joyous and carefree. We might try to hide from or outrun all that is frustrating and painful. Knowledge of the future might stunt our spiritual growth.

For more than three years, I have served on a Meetinghouse Committee seeking discernment about whether to remain in our present church building or to build a new one at a different site. When I agreed to serve, I thought our corporate prayers would result in God "zapping" us with a noble buyer for our present building, a definite sign that we should move. That did not happen. Instead God seemed to say, "I leave it to you to make the decision within the context of prayer. If you stay, *I'll be with you.* If you move, *I'll be with you.* Though not the answer we expected, it is, nevertheless, a wonderful promise!

As we moved through the process, church members weighed the nostalgic tug of a hundred-year-old building against the financial reality of remodeling and maintaining it. The call of stewardship moved us toward serious consideration of relocating. One member brought to us a vision along with a generous challenge of matching funds and a donation of land should we decide to move. After much prayer and discussion, Friends decided to take a leap of faith and build a more modest and functional church home in a new location. Only after we made the decision did God "zap" us with the jolting news that our ancient trusses had failed, slowly letting our roof down, and that the bricks, looking so sturdy from the outside, were bulging and crumbling on the inside. Our beautiful, spacious worship room was declared off limits! To our dismay the bids we received for repairs and bringing the building up to code were more than the amount needed to build a new meetinghouse! For a while, we worshiped in a new spirit of intimacy in our church library. Then when our church building was sold, the Beth Boruk Synagogue invited us to worship in their temple for as long as it took to build our new meetinghouse. Thirty-five years ago they had met for worship in our church while their temple was under construction. We feel God's grace blessing this generous arrangement with our Jewish brothers and sisters.

The primary object of this difficult search was to find the best location to carry out God's call to ministry and to follow God's leading. The Meetinghouse Committee represents the diversity of our congregation and its journey has been long and, at times, painful. Because of corporate and personal prayers, we have come to a sense of the meeting for new direction, and though we've struggled, our decisions have been made with little contention. To be able to carry out present and future ministries, our congregation made a commitment to raise enough money to move into a debt-free building. God and our members have been faithful to this promise. We recently had a groundbreaking ceremony on land fronting Friends Fellowship Community, a retirement home founded by Quakers. We expect to worship in our new meetinghouse in late 1998.

To be a seeker is to listen more than to speak. To be a seeker means to be intentional and diligent and patient in daily prayer, preparation, and persistence—trusting more in the unseen promises of God than in the seductions of the world.

The search flexes our spiritual muscles and nourishes our souls. The search not only offers guidance—it prepares us for the eternal encounter—standing awestruck in God's holy light—when we know we have found what we have been seeking.

A Soul in Search of Itself

Deep within us all there is an amazing inner sanctuary of the soul,
a holy place, a Divine Center, a speaking Voice, to which we may
continuously return. . . Yielding to these persuasions, gladly committing
ourselves. . .utterly and completely to the Light Within,
is the beginning of true life.
Thomas R. Kelly

Enormous emphasis is placed on the search for self. "To thine own self be true" has become an American commandment. Seminary students take personality inventories to find out who they are. When we make friends or think about a marriage partner, we look for "soul mates"—someone compatible with us. The search is valuable to our spiritual growth as long as we stay "in touch with that inner center." The tricky part is to meld the delicate spiritual balance of self with soul.

Part of my search for self takes place in my private devotions—in prayer and listening. We deny self when we try to live up to others' expectations. Indulging in harsh criticism of others, or our selves, is in effect criticizing God's creation. Developing a healthy ego frees us to discover God's intentions for us.

The other part of my search for self takes place in community. Good stewardship demands that I make consistent spiritual investments in my communities; family, faith, friendships, prayer, professional, study, and fellowship groups. Reaching out to others enlarges our self-concept of who we are and who we can become. It allows us to yield to divine impulses—affirming and loving others as well as ourselves. In community we are held together by a feeling of belonging to God, to Christ, and to each other.

Later in these essays I relate my struggles to develop my self-worth. Though I thank God daily for a sturdy physique, prayers to subdue my wayward appetite continue. However, prayers for my soul have been answered in amazing ways, including prayers I've not yet prayed! In God's infinite wisdom, I am given what I need, instead of what I want.

During the search for self, we do not journey alone. We have a Divine Companion—an Encourager, a Guide, and a Comforter. When we finally discover ourselves—our whole selves—we find our holy selves—as we come soul-to-Soul with our Creator.

Disciplines of the Spirit

*Now discipline always seems painful rather than pleasant
at the time, but later it yields the peaceful fruit of
righteousness to those who have been trained by it.*
Hebrews 12:11 NRSV

Discipline—often the very sight or sound of this word evokes
a strong reaction. The rebel in me wants little to do with discipline—it might invade the edges of my comfort zone. Yet the
adventurer in me is immediately intrigued by the possibilities
that may await at the next bend in my journey. But spiritual
disciplines, with their infinite dimensions, seem like a very special invitation from God.

The formation of my personal disciplines has been nurtured
by people, and by events—most recently, by a diagnosis of dia-
betes. Grateful for my earlier lessons in discipline, I know my
future good health depends on adhering to a sensible program of nutrition and exercise. *And I know that all disciplines
are spiritual.*

Memories I gladly recall that nurtured my spiritual disciplines include fellowship groups, retreats, worship, Sunday
school classes, Bible studies, leadership training, Stephen Ministry, and work camps, to mention only a few. More important
are warm recollections of drawing nearer to God as well as to
those who have intersected and joined my life journey.

Practice of spiritual disciplines moves us closer to God and to one another. In July 1989 when our granddaughter Hallie was born, we praised God for this wondrous blessing. The fruits of spiritual disciplines only multiplied our joy and heightened our awareness of the miracle of birth!

Spiritual disciplines, enhanced by the company of other seekers, prepare us for the event in life we most dread and least understand—death. In April 1991 when our son Bob died from leukemia, our community of faith helped us find solace in the midst of sorrow. We do not make our grief journey alone.

These two events in our family history caught us up in the sweep of humankind throughout the ages. We felt more than ever a part of the fabric of God's plan —connected to every other person in the universe. We felt caught up in the timeless words of scripture. "For everything there is a season, and a time for every matter under heaven: a time to be born, and a time to die. . . ." Ecclesiastes 3:1-2

The practice of spiritual disciplines—creative use of time, prayer, Scripture reading, meditation, solitude, worship, and mentoring—seems an ongoing gift as well as a personal invitation from God.

BODY AND SOUL

*I do not understand my own actions, for
I do not do what I want, but I do
the very thing I hate. . .*
Romans 7:15 NRSV

Born on a Saturday noon in December, I weighed in at more than eight pounds—a difficult delivery for my mother and the start of a life-long weight problem for me.

Mother gave up teaching to stay home with me. Dad, a builder, could find no work in those Depression days. In financial desperation, we accepted the offer to live with my uncle and aunt in their two-bedroom bungalow. Uncle Bob was a dentist with a nearby office, and Aunt Ruth was an elementary teacher. Mother kept house and cooked for the five of us. Dad finally found work as a driver of a dairy truck. Even with pooled resources, money was tight and food was precious. The mainstay of our diet was oxtail soup and leftover dairy products which Dad was allowed to bring home—whole milk, butter, cheese, and ice cream—delicious, calorie-laden (who was counting then?) but free!

Even as a toddler there were foods I rejected. Often, sitting at my little table, I fell asleep while sobbing in defiance, refusing to eat stewed tomatoes or being nauseated by the scent and taste of citrus. I liked smooth food, with no strings or seeds—I don't know why. Mother, like most mothers, felt compelled to make me clean up my plate. Because my aunt and uncle paid for the food, my behavior was wasteful and an embarrassment. Dad finally intervened, advising mother to give me alternative foods which I would not shun,

As a youngster I didn't understand "the Depression" nor how indebted we were to our relatives. Only as an adult did I begin to understand the graciousness of my aunt and uncle, and to realize what a blow it was to my parents' pride and desire for independence to have a child and no regular income. After ten months, Dad found a job in construction and we moved into a small home of our own. To thank my aunt and uncle for their kindness, Dad remodeled our former bedroom into a dental office and waiting room and built a garage as well.

Good days lay ahead—Dad found a job in construction and had a weekly paycheck, Mother was a good cook, and food was plentiful. I knew that I looked like my mother, a pleasant-looking woman, because everyone said so. We both had bright auburn hair and a smattering of freckles. One night we went to Dad's band concert. I sat wiggling around between my mother and my cousin. Each of them gave me a powder compact to play with to keep me still. Just before the house lights dimmed, I caught sight of my profile for the first time—and began quietly crying in the dark. My profile caught me unawares—it looked just like my dad, a nice-looking man. But I imagined I looked like the Breck shampoo girl with the turned-up nose that was in Mother's magazines! This discovery was a blow to a vanity that I didn't know I had. I wouldn't explain my tears, for my disappointment might seem disloyal.

My parents were intelligent, gregarious people who were fun to be around. I, an only child, did not enjoy the Sunday afternoon visits with my great-aunts and great-uncles. All dressed up, I was supposed to be seen but not heard. And there were murmurs, as if I couldn't hear, about whether I would lose my baby fat when I got older. It was a difficult time to be a little girl. In the movies Shirley Temple was tap-dancing her way into the hearts of the American public. Little Princess Elizabeth, on the pages of *Life* magazine, managed to look poised and perfect, even on horseback. They were role models I couldn't begin to imitate.

Dad maintained his weight because of daily physical activity. Mother kept losing, and regaining, the same twenty pounds, until she stabilized in her late sixties. I remember Mother's diets. She and I would faithfully eat controlled portions of food and do nightly exercises. She would lose twenty pounds and I would lose about five. Then we celebrated by going to Craig's Ice Cream Emporium in downtown Indianapolis to eat Persian Nut sundaes. As a youngster, I loved going off Mother's diet!

As I grew taller, I became scrawny—the only time in my life I weighed less than the insurance company graphs. All of my girlfriends had blossoming bosoms and I was flat as a board. Concerned about my slow passage into womanhood, Mother asked our family doctor what to do. Portly Dr. Wise gave us some of his own medicine—just add a big milkshake to my daily diet and in no time I would look like my friends. My hips and thighs blossomed, too much, and my bust blossomed two years later at its appointed time. In the meantime I was developing a weight problem.

When I was thirteen, my parents had a serious falling out— which they never discussed with me. All I knew was that they were very unhappy with each other and didn't speak for twelve interminable months. At the dinner table they spoke only to me. Thankfully money was still tight, so Dad did not move out. Mother explained that when we were out in public we were to keep up appearances and no one—NO ONE—was to be told what was happening.

I shed a good many tears in private in God's presence, for God was the only friend available to talk to. I always felt blessed that at about age four, through church and Sunday school and kindly parents, I understood that I could be myself in God's presence. There was no need to hide any part of myself, for as my Creator, God knew me fully. This is one of the greatest gifts of grace I have ever received. Pouring out my feelings to God about the inexplicable pain of our family troubles was my only release.

Out of frustration, I discovered that eating gave me comfort and temporarily filled a nameless void. I knew my parents loved me, but sensing that they no longer loved each other filled me with fear and dread. With no explanation of what was happening, I somehow felt responsible. Had I looked like a movie star or a princess, maybe this never would have happened. God and food became constant companions—to ease the sorrow and confusion I felt.

After more than a year, my parents gradually made up—it took another year for trust to be reestablished. I was now fifteen and plump. Mother was still privately consulting friends and relatives about the possibility of my becoming slender. Food took on a different dynamic—not only was it a source of fleeting comfort but now guilt and shame about any food I ate overcame me. I didn't know what to do and couldn't find the words or courage to share my feelings with my parents. Though plump, my high school years were happy—good friends, good grades, and lots of activities.

As a freshman at Earlham College, in Richmond, Indiana, I immediately felt at home and soon had a circle of friends. There were challenging classes with interesting professors, a choir to sing in, a campus newspaper to write for, and my first introduction to Quakerism. My original roommate and I did not bond—I think they only matched us because we were both large women. Stuart (Mary Stuart, that is) carried her weight with boldness, was sophisticated beyond her years, and had enough self-assurance for six people. We definitely didn't have anything in common! I found kindred spirits in my dorm, my classes, and in several Christian fellowship groups. Despite starchy cafeteria food, my weight stabilized because I walked everywhere.

My sophomore year I met my future husband John, a day student, and after graduation we married. I was as happy and self-confident then as at any period in my life. My weight was at its lowest—though I thought I was still too heavy. Surprised to find I had no passion for cooking (I thought it came with the vows), still I enjoyed preparing meals for my new husband. In my contentment additional pounds were added.

Two years later, with my physician's encouragement, I gained quite a few pounds with my first pregnancy, learning six weeks before delivery to expect twins. After Leslie and Lynn's birth, I lost only part of that weight. Two-and-a-half years later our son Bob joined our family and five years later Laura was born. The pounds accumulated after each pregnancy. I was now at an unhealthy weight and sorely disturbed about it.

God patiently listened to me and I patiently *tried* to listen to God. . . .

Body and SOUL

No one can call me inferior without my consent.
Eleanor Roosevelt

For the next six years, to paraphrase the opening lines of *A Tale of Two Cities,* it was the brightest of times and the bleakest of times. It was bright because I loved being a wife and mother. It was a joy to help our babies develop into interesting and creative children. It was bleak because I was consumed with low self-esteem, guilt for being so heavy, and total frustration in dealing with it. I never wanted to look like a movie star or a princess. What I most wanted was to be *unremarkable.* I longed *not* to stand out in a crowd. With bright auburn hair and too many pounds, I was hardly inconspicuous. In addition to my lack of self-confidence, I began to withdraw from social contact, except for my family and a few close friends. I sang in the church choir, thankful for a robe that helped me blend in with others. I was so absorbed in imagining another person's unspoken judgment of me that I lost my natural ability to converse. In my self-conscious state I imagined them thinking, "She's got no will power." "Doesn't she care how she looks?" "Such pretty hair, if only she'd lose some weight." I dreaded meeting anyone new and crossed to the other side of the street to avoid speaking to acquaintances. I even felt uncomfortable with my in-laws, most of whom were naturally slender.

I didn't fit the cultural norm. It was frustrating to live in a Twiggy world with a Rubenesque body. Stylish clothing for large women wasn't yet on the drawing board, so I rotated three dark outfits to fit all occasions. Unlike other mothers, I didn't fit into the little chairs when I visited my children's classroom. My first concern when flying was whether the seatbelt would fasten comfortably. I scouted out the furniture wherever I visited, avoiding spindly antiques or upholstered pieces that would swallow me. I viewed my life through "fat" lenses.

My husband was a good listener and only concerned for my well-being. Though he cherished me and never judged me, he couldn't understand the intensity of my feelings. As Karl Menninger, M.D., says, "It is hard for a free fish to understand what is happening to a hooked one." I was so driven by shame and self-loathing that it was difficult to fully appreciate the love and strength of our family life.

I had a problem that I didn't know how to fix. I'm a list-maker, a problem-solver, and a doer. But losing weight doesn't happen with one decision on a list. It requires many decisions on a daily basis for a lifetime. And dieting was more "not do-ing" than "doing." When Lynn and Leslie were about two, I talked with my pastor, who was also a good friend, about my feelings of frustration. He thought if I concentrated on the positives in my life, that it would minimize my negative feel-ings. The only thing I remember about the personal traits and gifts test that he gave me was that I worked best when focused on one thing at a time—we laughed together at the irony—this was not good news for the mother of twins!

The years sped by. I was at ease at home and with a few friends, but avoided the agony of meeting anyone new. I prayed fervently for guidance, sometimes cried when alone, and ate everything in sight to stifle my ambivalent feelings. In retro-spect, I think I was praying amiss—I was really only worrying in the presence of God.

My prayers were answered in an unexpected way. God gave me what I needed rather than what I wanted. One evening during my devotions, a message came with a jolt. *Suppose that you never achieve your goal in weight loss. How long are you going to concentrate on the negatives, while ignoring all the pluses in your life? When are you going to claim all that you are and start **living**?"* That really got my attention! My transformation began immediately. With God's help I began to cast out the demons of shame, blame, and guilt, and accepted personal responsibility for who I had become and for who I wanted to be.

I timidly began serving on several church committees and soon was asked to take leadership roles. With an agenda in hand and Kingdom business to attend to, I chaired a number of groups. Church seemed like a safe place to begin living again. It was now the height of the civil rights movement and things were heating up in Richmond, especially at the high school. Several members of our church were approached to study and to put into practice group conversation techniques to ease racial tensions. This method, called Quaker dialogue, was developed by a Friend from New Jersey, Rachel Davis DuBois. Impressed with her books, I decided to take the training with several others.

The concept of Quaker dialogue is to gather a diverse group of people, twelve to sixteen in number, and by a series of questions begin to build trust within the group. Then we could start to discuss honestly and openly the issues of fear and mistrust that separated us. We began with a nonthreatening universal kind of question, going around the circle with everyone participating: "Where were you born?" or "Please share an early memory of your childhood kitchen." Gradually the questions moved to a deeper level with persons sharing as they wished: "What was your first day of school like?" and moving to "How old were you when you first became aware of discrimination?" More specific questions moved us toward exchanging ideas about how to improve communication and racial relationships at the high school and in our community. After two or three sessions trust was high, discussions centered on the heart of the problems, and creative solutions began to emerge.

The success of this dialogue was energizing and exciting. An additional bonus was my growing self-confidence and re-discovery of the art of conversation. Now suddenly, engrossed in Kingdom work and the techniques learned in Quaker dia-logue, I was liberated to interact naturally with anyone I met, even strangers. In the forgetting of self, the barriers of self-inflicted judgment and misery rolled away. My weight had only improved a little, but I felt much lighter, for God restored my soul and freed me from bondage.

Our children were growing up and I was thankful for all the years I had at home to nurture them. I began to consider finding interesting part-time work. I had two interviews in the field of interior design. Both positions were offered, but after much prayer I declined. Several months later an explosion caused by gun powder and leaking gas destroyed much of down-town Richmond. Both stores in which I considered working were leveled and lives were lost. I was grateful that I had waited for a spiritual leading.

Two years later I received a phone call asking me to inter-view for a position as part-time assistant to the editor of *Quaker Life,* the denominational magazine for Friends United Meet-ing. The job was offered and accepted, and for the next eight years I worked mornings, savoring my editorial duties and feel-ing that I had found a niche for my gifts and interests. The opportunity to work full time with the magazine came just as our youngest daughter Laura was going off to college in Iowa. The work was both absorbing and challenging, thanks largely to the four editors with whom I was associated. I retired as managing editor at the end of 1994.

Meanwhile, what was happening with my body? Once in my thirties, once in my forties, and once in my fifties, I lost a great deal of weight quickly and in an unhealthy way. I could not maintain the loss so I gained it all back because I had not yet re-educated my eating habits.

Now in retirement, I still deal daily with my life-long nemesis—food, my friend *and* my enemy. Though no longer obsessed with my weight, I am concerned about my health. After so many years of yo-yo dieting, my body no longer signals satiety. My body structure is still just like that of my paternal grandmother Kate. I take medication for hypertension and was recently diagnosed as a non-insulin dependent diabetic. I adhere to a sensible diet, work out aerobically three times a week (still looking for that elusive or missing athletic gene!), and continue to pray for physical healing. Each one-fourth pound loss is a victory. No more quick unhealthy fixes for me—I'm trying to improve the rest of my life.

My self-esteem and self-confidence are built on the rock of my God-given talents and abilities. Daily I thank God for my sturdy body, instead of complaining, and try to eat wisely just for that day.

I think that if in heaven we are all Spirit, it will be a relief to quit counting calories and stepping on scales. I hope with all my heart what St. John of the Cross says is true: "In the twilight of life, God will not judge us on our earthly possessions and human success, but rather on how much we have loved." On that basis, I might weigh in O.K.

BEETHOVEN ON COMPUTER

All as God wills, who wisely heeds
To give or to withhold,
And knoweth more of all my needs
Than all my prayers have told.
John Greenleaf Whittier

Richard was born February 2, 1951. At age seven he was diagnosed with muscular dystrophy, a genetic disorder causing a progressive deterioration of the muscles. Much about the disease was a mystery to the doctors, but there were dire predictions, most of which have come true.

At age twelve Richard began playing the piano—practicing for hours, much as his idol Ludwig van Beethoven did, until he played the piece perfectly. He took lessons at a nearby conservatory and at age fifteen gave his first recital, which brought a standing ovation. His natural talent included an extraordinary ear for pitch, sound, and tempo.

By the age of twenty he was no longer able to play the piano. By age twenty-one he was in a wheelchair permanently, experiencing daily an agonizing deterioration of his muscles. Excursions with family and friends became less frequent, then became impossible.

At age thirty-seven Richard became very ill. Hospitalized for four months, he was put on a mechanical respirator. When released, he received home nursing care. Later on he became quadriplegic, necessitating around-the-clock care. He is presently in the last stages of the disease, which was originally thought to be Duchenne muscular dystrophy, with a life expectancy of twenty years. Now doctors suspect that he has another form called Becker's, which has a longer life span. Richard can move his head from side to side but cannot move from the neck down. During the day, a nurse along with a college student cares for him. At night, the person with whom he shares an apartment or, on occasion, his parents who live in other cities are at his side.

With physical deterioration came a downward spiral into despair. At age thirty-seven, Richard didn't get out of bed for a year because it seemed he had nothing to live for. Finally, with the continuing encouragement of family and friends and the help of anti-depressants, he once again left his bed for part of the day. He established a routine of reading, listening to music, and using his computer to write to family and friends—but still felt there was no purpose to life—he was just going through the limited motions from day to day.

During all his struggles with growing physical limitations, Richard didn't indulge in self-pity. But through the years the store of anger grew until he exploded in frustration, lashing out at those around him. The unremitting pain he felt, he saw reflected in the eyes of those who loved him. Could anything make living worthwhile again?

In 1992, life took on new possibilities when Richard learned of the Musical Instrument Digital Interface program (MIDI) introduced by the State of Michigan and the Learning Resource Center in Lansing. Richard's passion for music was about to be rekindled through the MIDI computer program. In simple terms (simpler for those who use computers than for those who don't!) the MIDI interface card attaches inside so the computer can talk to a synthesizer which contains digital samples of real live piano. The computer and the synthesizer are hooked up to stereo equipment.

Richard first had to learn Morse Code. By use of dots and dashes, he sips and puffs on a plastic tube to transcribe notes onto a computer monitor. Then it is played through his stereo equipment. He is concentrating on making tapes of the solo piano works of Beethoven, his mentor, who was also physically challenged. For the last two years he has been selling tapes of his version of some of Beethoven's works.

The tedious process of MIDI takes about 1,000 hours per piece. He spends about five hours a day in transcription. The result is incredible! At first one might imagine Beethoven himself at the keyboard, but Richard melds his own interpretation with the style of the master.

Richard is interested in serving music, not technology. Through MIDI editing over a long period of time, and listening carefully, the tape is gradually refined. He copies the score into the computer, letting it read Beethoven in strict tempo; then Richard spends many painstaking hours at fine-tuning. In his own words, "I don't want this means of realized performance to replace playing the piano the usual way. It can't and it won't. What I am doing is research into the most interesting body of piano music ever written by anyone." Presenting a computerized recital in the future is his next goal.

Finding an outlet for his musical gifts and passions defuses much of the anger and frustration. "Playing the piano" once again nurtures Richard's creative soul. Each day holds enticing musical options. Richard, Beethoven, and a computer— an unlikely alliance and a unique answer to prayer—form an incredible network of expectation and fulfillment!

An Electric Moment

Coincidences are God's way of remaining anonymous.
G. Peter Fleck

John and I had just finished registering at a beautiful city camp-ground on the outskirts of St. Louis. It was a balmy April week-day—with only fifty or sixty tents and campers scattered across the sprawling meadow. It was spring break and we were look-ing forward to a mini-vacation with our thirteen-year-old daugh-ter Laura.

As we came out of the office, a middle-aged man in a pick-up truck gestured to us. He and the man riding with him were strangers. The driver said, "Your camper caught on fire; your daughter is safe; the fire's out." Without another word he drove off, leaving us to follow on foot as fast as we could.

We found Laura comfortably seated at a nearby camper. We were told that the refrigerator wiring in our rented RV had shorted out. After giving our neighbors profuse thanks for their assistance, we went back to clean up the mess and trans-fer the food into our coolers. Then our daughter told us the details.

Laura had developed a nasty cold while we were traveling west. Medicine had not yet taken effect; her head was stuffy and she could hardly breathe. All day long food had seemed unappealing, so she decided to stay in the camper and try to eat some fresh strawberries while we signed in. She sat down at the table in the forward part of the camper with her back to the refrigerator. She was totally unaware of the sparks igniting behind her. Only when someone pounded on the door yelling "fire" did she realize something was wrong. She hurriedly escaped by the front door of the camper as the stranger came in the rear door with an extinguisher and put out the flames.

Later that evening, we visited with our neighbors who invited us to join them around the campfire. Our initial shock over Laura's narrow escape had been immediately replaced by thankfulness to God and to the alert stranger who had saved our daughter's life.

But I had a question for our good samaritan. Our camper door faced away from his camper—how, when the campers were all preparing their evening meals—grilling this, barbecuing that—did this man know our camper was on fire? He and his wife looked at each other. With a warm smile she said, "It's his job to smell the difference; he's the fire chief of Oklahoma City!"

Souvenir of Color

God has no favorites, let us have none.
Anonymous

The spring before I was to graduate, the Earlham College Department of Community Relations organized its first overseas work camp—a bold venture for 1949. The student group—six women and six men, eleven of us white, and Leonard, black—traveled with two leaders to the island of Jamaica. We would spend the summer rebuilding a flood-ravaged church on higher ground.

Following a two-day drive to Florida, we spent six hours in the Miami airport. We then flew to Kingston, where unfamiliar but friendly folks greeted us at the airport and helped move us through customs.

The tropical heat was oppressive as we climbed into a battered mission van, settling down anywhere we could amidst too many people and too much luggage. The beauty of the changing turquoise hues of the Caribbean and the lushness of the flowers and trees offered some distraction from the van's rapid rate of speed as we traveled toward the city. Driving on the left side of the road, we seemed to be playing "chicken" with assorted autos, pedestrians, dogs, and strutting roosters. There were no accidents, just one-a-minute close calls!

Signs of poverty were evident all around us—in contrast to the estates dotting the hillside some miles away. We passed a fascinating array of people, including children, whose expressive faces reflected every skin color imaginable.

Soon we left the crowded streets of the city. The roads narrowed and curved around the hillsides as we drove to the village of Buff Bay. Our speed never slowed, but the blaring of horns alerted oncoming drivers, as well as other moving obstacles in the road. It was still daylight and we were all excited and a little bit anxious. The driver started singing hymns, mostly familiar but with a different beat. We soon joined in, praying that "When We All Get to Heaven" would not be a divine summons as we careened around each curve with darkening ravines on one side.

It was dusk by the time we reached the house where the women would live. Charles Vincent, a Jamaican pastor, and his wife Mabel were to be our hosts. Both were East Indians who had gone to college in the United States. They, with their five shy young sons, greeted us warmly, with kerosene lamps to light our way. Although there was no electricity, we were glad that this simple but hospitable home had indoor plumbing! We settled into a dorm-like room, actually the Vincents' living room, while the men in our group were taken to their quarters, two doors away.

Our time in Jamaica was memorable. A cock's crow was our alarm clock. Early each weekday we traveled twelve miles in the back of a truck to the church site in Dover. Sometimes we made gravel by pounding rocks; often we shoveled endless piles of sand; and other times we hauled buckets of water to make cement. When the base of the foundation was finally complete, despite the heat of the afternoon sun, we and our Jamaican helpers danced a high-spirited Virginia Reel to tamp down the gravel. Then we all cooled off by sucking a stalk of sugar cane—a very sweet but welcome refreshment.

We experienced a hard-working, perspiration-laden summer complete with sunburn and insect bites, but also filled with singing and laughter, fellowship with Jamaicans and with each other. Early on Saturdays we walked to the town market to barter for food and souvenirs. Later we swam and picnicked and strolled on the beach or climbed waterfalls. On Sundays we attended worship and gave programs to help raise money for building supplies. Sunday afternoons were leisurely and very British as we visited the homes of neighboring Friends who prepared lavish high teas.

The Vincent family became our family, as we ate together and helped with household chores. What a treat to step into the yard to pick ripe mangoes, bananas, and pineapples for our nightly meal! Most evenings we gathered around a little pump organ in the dining room singing Jamaican songs and trying to learn the dialect called *patois*. Before retiring, we often sat on the veranda to talk or to watch fireflies sparkling in the dark.

The weeks sped by and work on the church progressed slowly. But by summer's end the foundation was complete and the first-floor columns were in place. Too soon it was time to leave. Our hearts were bursting with gratitude for the generosity of the Jamaican friends we had met, especially the Vincents. And our hearts burst, too, with sadness at the idea of saying goodbye.

We were a thoughtful and subdued group of young people as we prepared to return to the States. We had become immersed in a totally new culture and now were reluctant to leave. Would we ever see our new friends again once we left the island? Would we even see one another again as we moved on to new destinations and careers?

Forty-nine years later, my most vivid recollection of that trip is as fresh as the day it happened—a memory that pierced our hearts in Florida and made our hearts rejoice in Jamaica.

Of the twelve Americans in our work camp, eleven of us were white. Leonard was black. In the shelter of our campus we were a closeknit group. On the way to Jamaica, during the six-hour wait in Miami airport in pre-civil rights days, the "coloreds only" signs and the "whites only" signs everywhere fragmented our group. The waiting rooms, restaurants, drinking fountains, and restrooms were clearly marked.

The contrast when we landed in Kingston was amazing! Eleven of us were in the minority but we were not despised or segregated. And Leonard immediately felt at home. For an entire summer we were just a group of twelve; racism was not an intruder. We worked together, ate together, and worshiped together. In rare times of relaxation, in youthful exuberance we often held hands as we jumped into the surf or strolled along the pristine sandy beaches.

I always think of the summer of 1949 in Jamaica as "Paradise found" —TOGETHER!

EPILOGUE

Life is a collection of moments. As faithful stewards we are asked to examine these moments—to receive spiritual guidance from the blessings, the cautions, and the energy that our moments have to offer.

In the words of Herb Mather, "God calls us to be good stewards of all that we are and all that we have. . .biblical stewardship has to do with how we manage *everything* in life as a trust from God. . . ."

What is our Spirit-led human response to our God-given resources? I believe our answers will illumine our spiritual journey in fresh and exciting ways!

CWB

Chagares Photography, Richmond, Indiana

ABOUT THE AUTHOR

A native of Indianapolis, Ind., Carol Beals is a graduate of Earlham College. For almost twenty-five years she was associated with *Quaker Life,* the denominational magazine for Friends United Meeting. She retired as managing editor in December 1994.

Co-recipient of the Patrick Henry Memorial Christian Writer's Scholarship at the Earlham School of Religion, Richmond, she wrote *Cheerful Giving* & *Kingdom Living* as part of the discipline for the award. These devotional essays reflect the author's belief and practice that we are stewards of *everything* God gives us.

With a more relaxed schedule, she enjoys making fabric wall hangings, camping and travel, as well as free-lance editing. Carol and her land surveyor husband John are the parents of four and grandparents of three. They are long-time members of First Friends Meeting in Richmond.

NOTES

NOTES

NOTES

NOTES